Straight Talk About...
SUICIDE

Rachel
Eagen

Crabtree Publishing Company
www.crabtreebooks.com

Developed and produced by: Plan B Book Packagers

Editorial director: Ellen Rodger

Art director: Rosie Gowsell-Pattison

Fictional Introductions: Rachel Eagen

Editor: Molly Aloian

Project coordinator: Kathy Middleton

Production coordinator: Margaret Amy Salter

Prepress technician: Margaret Amy Salter

Consultant: Susan Rodger, PhD., C. Psych.,
Psychologist and Professor Faculty of Education,
The University of Western Ontario

Photographs:
Title page: Nick S./Shutterstock Inc.; p. 4: Leah-Anne
Thompson/Shutterstock Inc.; p. 6: Kwest/Shutterstock
Inc.; p. 8: Laurin Rinder/Shutterstock Inc.; p. 10: N.

Marques74/Shutterstock Inc.; p. 11: Creativemarc/
iStockPhoto.com; p. 12: Soul Of Autumn | Vladimir
Konovalov/Shutterstock Inc.; p. 14: (left) 66North/
iStockPhoto.com, (bottom) Monkey Business Images/
Shutterstock Inc.; p. 16: Gemenacom/Shutterstock Inc.;
p. 17: Christy Thompson/Shutterstock Inc.; p. 18:
photomak/Shutterstock Inc.; p. 20: Kevin Carden/
Shutterstock Inc.; p. 23: Iodrakon/Shutterstock Inc.;
p. 24 (bottom): Aquaspects/Shutterstock Inc.,
(left) iQoncept/Shutterstock Inc.; p. 25: Nigel Paul
Monckton/Shutterstock Inc.; p. 26: Mila Supinskaya/
Shutterstock Inc.; p. 28: Wallenrock/Shutterstock Inc.;
p. 29: PhotoSmart/Shutterstock Inc.; p. 30: Amid/
Shutterstock Inc.; p. 31: Lisa F. Young/Shutterstock Inc.;
p. 32: Yan Zenkis/Shutterstock Inc.; p. 34: @erics/
Shutterstock Inc.; p. 35: Halima Ahkdar/Shutterstock
Inc.; p. 36: Dave Thompson/Shutterstock Inc.; p. 38:
Ivar/iStockPhoto.com; p. 39: Sander Crombeen/
Shutterstock Inc.; p. 40: Petrenko Andriy/Shutterstock
inc.; p. 41: Naluwan/Shutterstock Inc.; p. 42: Denis
Tabler/Shutterstock Inc.

Library and Archives Canada Cataloguing in Publication

Eagen, Rachel, 1979-
   Suicide / Rachel Eagen.

(Straight talk about--)
Includes index.
Issued also in an electronic format.
ISBN 978-0-7787-2131-4 (bound).--ISBN 978-0-7787-2138-3 (pbk.)

   1. Suicide--Juvenile literature. 2. Suicide--Prevention--
Juvenile literature. I. Title. II. Series: Straight talk about--
(St. Catharines, Ont.)

HV6546.E23 2010   j362.28   C2010-902893-7

Library of Congress Cataloging-in-Publication Data

Eagen, Rachel.
  Suicide / Rachel Eagen.
      p. cm. -- (Straight talk about--)
  Includes index.
  ISBN 978-0-7787-2138-3 (pbk. : alk. paper) --
  ISBN 978-0-7787-2131-4 (reinforced library binding : alk. paper)
  -- ISBN 978-1-4271-9544-9 (electronic (pdf))
  1. Suicide--Juvenile literature. 2. Suicide--Prevention--Juvenile
literature. 3. Youth--Suicidal behavior--Juvenile literature.
  I. Title. II. Series.

  HV6546.E24 2011
  616.85'8445--dc22
                                        2010017139

Crabtree Publishing Company

www.crabtreebooks.com   1-800-387-7650

Printed in Hong Kong/042011/BK20110304

Published in Canada
Crabtree Publishing
616 Welland Ave.
St. Catharines, ON
L2M 5V6

Published in the United States
Crabtree Publishing
PMB 59051
350 Fifth Avenue, 59th Floor
New York, NY 10118

Published in the United Kingdom
Crabtree Publishing
Maritime House
Basin Road North, Hove
BN41 1WR

Published in Australia
Crabtree Publishing
386 Mt. Alexander Rd.
Ascot Vale (Melbourne)
VIC 3032

CONTENTS

The backpack was heavy on Anthony's shoulders. It was full of books and homework, and the math test with the fat red zero on it. The teacher had drawn a sad face inside the hollow, empty number. Beside it, she had written: What happened?

It was a good question, but Anthony didn't have the answer. He didn't know the answer to anything anymore. Nothing made sense. School was a joke. If it wasn't enough that he was flunking out, there was the fact that no one wanted to talk to him. It was like they were afraid of catching a disease or something. Or maybe they blamed him. He could see the fear in their eyes. Jack's friend. Had it really only been six months?

Anthony was with him when he died. A tangle of tubes and wires fed him and helped him breathe. During the last month he was too weak to play cards or watch television, so Anthony had just sat and talked to him. He told him what he was missing in school, and that baseball tryouts weren't the same without him. Sad-faced nurses told Anthony how brave he was, and what a good friend. Anthony didn't feel brave at all.

Everyone said that it would take time to feel better, but Anthony didn't believe it. He didn't even want to feel better anymore. How could he feel better? How was he supposed to go on without his best friend? How could he even live? Lately it seemed like it would be better just to end it all.

Introduction
Heavy Heart

Anthony is struggling with thoughts of suicide, likely brought on by an illness called depression. There can be different reasons for what makes a person think about ending his or her life. For Anthony, it is the stress of watching his friend get sick and die.

In this book, you will learn what drives people to commit suicide, as well as how suicide affects the people who are left behind. You can read about what puts people at a greater risk for suicide, and find out how to reach out to a friend in trouble.

"He didn't even leave a note. I thought that's what people do, they leave a note explaining why they did it. There was just nothing. One day he was alive and everything was cool and then he was dead. I didn't have a clue. I feel like I should have paid more attention."
Nathan, aged 16.

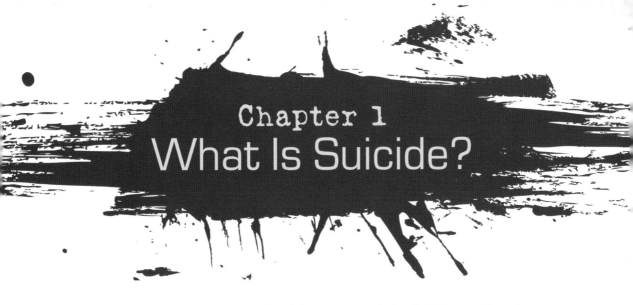

Chapter 1
What Is Suicide?

Suicide is when someone decides to end their life and takes action to die. The word suicide comes from two Latin words: *sui*, or of oneself, and *cidium*, or killing. Suicide is not a new **phenomenon**, but that does not make it any less upsetting for the people who lose someone in this way.

Silent Suffering

Most people have very strong thoughts and feelings about suicide. In many cultures, suicide is thought to be **morally** wrong. **Psychologists** believe that when a person chooses to die, it is because they have lost hope for a solution to their problems. It is an act made out of utter desperation. Sadly, many people who commit suicide cannot see the help that is available to them. Friends and family—the survivors—often realize too late just how badly their loved one was feeling. That does not mean that friends and family members are to blame for suicides, but most suicides are preventable. Talking about suicide is an important step toward helping people who feel they cannot be helped.

Who Commits Suicide?

In North America, teenagers are among the most **vulnerable** group of people for suicide. In fact, suicide is the third most common way that young people aged 15-24 die in the United States. Suicide rates among young adolescents, aged 10-14, are also rising. Over the past few decades, suicide rates have almost doubled for this age group. Both males and females attempt suicide, but statistics show that females attempt suicide three times more often than males. However, four out of five deaths by suicide are male. The reason for this is that males often attempt to end their lives using more violent methods, such as shooting or hanging themselves. Females are more likely to overdose on pills, which can allow more time for them to be saved.

Why Would Someone Do It?

It can be hard to understand why someone would choose to commit suicide. People who have suffered difficult or **traumatic** experiences might feel that it is the only way to end their suffering. It is important to keep in mind that people who commit suicide want to put an end to their pain, but that does not always mean that they want to stop living.

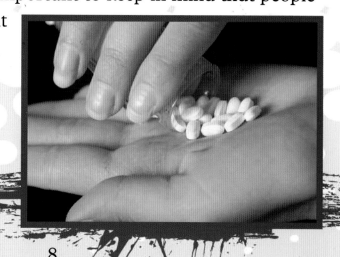

Girls are more likely to steal pills from relatives in suicide attempts.

The Why's of Suicide

Listed below are some well-known factors that can contribute to suicidal thoughts and feelings:

Family Problems
Difficulties at home can be very stressful. The breakup of a relationship between parents or losing a family member can also be very hard on the whole family. Emotional, physical, or sexual abuse at home can also lead to feelings of self-hatred and worthlessness, which can lead to suicidal thoughts over time.

Sexual Confusion
Teens who are coming to terms with their sexual identity may also struggle with suicidal thoughts, especially if they live in communities where being gay, lesbian, or bisexual is frowned upon.

Body Image Issues
Feeling bad about your body is called poor body image. Most teens feel bad about their bodies at some point. Over time, poor body image can lead to self-hatred, which can fuel suicidal feelings.

Pressures at School
Problems at school can range from struggling with grades or learning disabilities to feeling pressure to succeed. Many teens put a lot of pressure on themselves or have pressure placed on them by their parents. The expectations might be so high that teens feel like failures no matter how well they succeed. Social problems at school, such as bullying, or rejection by peers or dating partners, can be so humiliating for teens that they want to end their lives.

Dying by Accident

For many people, attempting suicide is a cry for help. It shows others that they are suffering and need support. Sometimes, a suicide attempt is a wake-up call to the people in that person's life. With the right treatment and support, people can recover and become happy again.

Unfortunately, not everyone who tries to commit suicide can be saved. That is why prevention is so important. Whether someone really wants to die or not, all people who are suicidal need help.

Depression

Depression is a common mental illness that affects many people. It can be a temporary problem or something that lasts longer. Some people struggle with depression their entire lives. It can be the result of **intense** life experiences, changes in the body, loss of relationships, illness, loneliness, or using drugs or alcohol. Some people are more likely to suffer from depression because of the way their brain works. Depression is a treatable illness. The trouble is that many people who experience depression feel too bad to seek help, which makes it worse. Depression can lead to suicidal behaviors when it is left untreated.

Depression alters how the brain works.

Risk Groups

Did you know that 15-to-24-year-olds suffer from the highest rate of depression in the world? Unfortunately, this age group is the least likely to seek help. There are several other high-risk groups for depression in North America. Aboriginal peoples in both the United States and Canada have high rates of depression and suicide, as well as Hispanic and Latino peoples, who may struggle with feelings of **isolation** and displacement—the feeling that you do not belong. It can be hard not to feel this way when most of the people around you are a different race or come from a different cultural background than you. This is especially true for new immigrants who may struggle with feelings of homesickness. Gay, lesbian, and bisexual youth are another high-risk group, as well as teens that are born with **Aspergers syndrome**. The feeling that you are all alone and that no one can help is a common feeling among people in these groups.

Gay teens are more at risk for suicide because they struggle with acceptance.

"Mostly I would think about how things would be better when I was gone, not about how I was going to do it. I just was tired of hurting all the time and I couldn't see how things would ever change."
Fantie, aged 17.

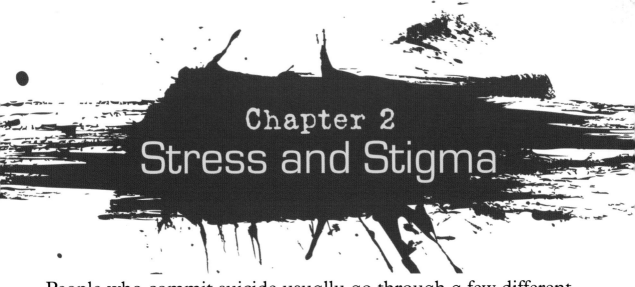

Chapter 2
Stress and Stigma

People who commit suicide usually go through a few different stages before they take action to end their lives. But that is not true for everyone. Some people kill themselves without thinking it through. A single upsetting event might lead a person to end their life before pursuing any options that might help them feel better.

Suicide Ideation

Psychologists use the term suicide ideation to describe suicidal thoughts and behaviors. The term ideation comes from the word idea, so suicide ideation means thoughts about killing yourself. Ideation does not necessarily mean that someone is moments away from attempting suicide. Some people simply wonder what the world would be like without them. They might have fantasies about what their funeral would be like and who would miss them the most. These thoughts, while they might sound unhealthy, are normal. Almost everyone experiences a form of suicide ideation at some point in their lives. Suicide ideation also includes making a plan to kill yourself, as well as unsuccessful suicide attempts.

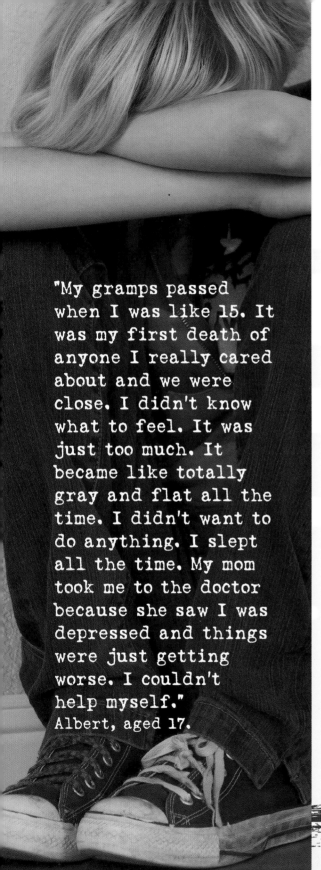

"My gramps passed when I was like 15. It was my first death of anyone I really cared about and we were close. I didn't know what to feel. It was just too much. It became like totally gray and flat all the time. I didn't want to do anything. I slept all the time. My mom took me to the doctor because she saw I was depressed and things were just getting worse. I couldn't help myself."
Albert, aged 17.

Bad Feelings

Psychologists who specialize in suicide talk about suicide as a process. It starts with bad feelings. These feelings can come from an upsetting life event, such as a breakup, the divorce of parents, death of a loved one, and big life changes, such as moving far away. Some people suffer from **mood disorders** that make them prone to bad feelings. That does not make them crazy. It just means that their brains naturally function in ways that are different from people who are described as having "normal" brain function.

Depression may make it difficult to get out of bed.

Darkness Falls

Feeling bad from time to time is part of being alive. We would not be human if we always felt happy, safe, and good about our lives. When bad things happen, it is natural to feel down. It might take a few days to start feeling better, but eventually, you start to get over whatever happened. Not everyone works this way. For some people, upsetting situations can lead them into a very dark period. They start to struggle with day-to-day life, and simple things, such as getting out of bed, going to school or work, and eating regular meals, become almost impossible. This is called depression. Most medical doctors and psychologists agree that a person who has been feeling very bad every day for most of the day for at least two weeks is depressed.

Making a Plan

People who are depressed need help to get better. Help might come in the way of talking to family or friends. It might also involve talking to a counselor, seeking other forms of **therapy**, or taking medication. Depression is nothing to be ashamed of, but many people who suffer from depression do not seek treatment. This is very dangerous, because once a person becomes depressed, they may start thinking of ways to escape their terrible feelings. It is at this point that a person might have their first thoughts of killing themselves. Suicide becomes an escape. This is when they think about how they will do it and when.

Breaking the Cycle

Feeling depressed, making a plan, and carrying it out are the three stages that most suicidal people go through. It is important to remember that the process can be stopped at any point. Most suicides are preventable, which is why it is so important to reach out to a person who is suffering. It is not the responsibility of others to stop a person from dying, but in a lot of cases, people have the power to change what happens in another person's life. Knowing how to read the warning signs of suicide can help save lives.

Strong Feelings

It is healthy to experience strong feelings. These feelings can be both positive and negative. Intense feelings of happiness make you feel like you can fly. Extremely upsetting feelings make you want to crawl into a hole. Responding emotionally to life is both normal and healthy. However, it is important to learn how to express emotions appropriately. This is especially

true for negative emotions. Dealing with emotions is not the same as dulling them. Dealing means **acknowledging** your feelings and letting them out in healthy ways. The ways that we deal with our emotions are called **coping mechanisms**. Coping with emotions is how we prevent them from getting out of control and ruling our lives.

Teens in Turmoil

It is a **stereotype** that all adolescents and teenagers are miserable. But there is a reason for the stereotype, because adolescence really is a difficult time. It is a period of intense change. The release of **hormones** fuel new emotions and abrupt mood swings, which can make you feel like you are losing your mind. Hormones are also responsible for changes in your body. Greasy hair and acne, which are signs that your hormones are doing their job, can make you feel **insecure** and unhappy with yourself. The bad news is that hormones are not the only thing that teens have to deal with. Many adolescents and teens also start high school, which is a strange new environment. It is also a place that might not seem as safe or **predictable** as elementary or middle school. Classes become more challenging, which is especially hard for students who struggle in certain subjects or who have learning disabilities. High school also signals new demands in friendships and dating relationships.

There are so many new emotional issues to deal with in your teen years.

"It's All my Fault"

A lot of adolescents and teens suffer in silence. They may blame themselves for their unhappiness or feel too embarrassed to ask for help. Social challenges, such as rejection by friends or dating partners, bullying, and peer pressure, can exaggerate feelings of worthlessness, which can make speaking up even harder. Many teens turn inward and try to handle their problems on their own. However, most lack the ability to cope because they do not have any experience in dealing with such intense emotions. For this reason, some teens turn to self-destructive coping mechanisms, such as abusing drugs or alcohol, and self-injury—cutting, burning, and hurting your body in other ways. Some adolescents and teens turn to the wrong people for support, such as abusive dating partners, which can make everything a lot worse.

Girls think about suicide more often but they are less likely to see it through than guys.

Suicide and Sexuality

Teens who are struggling with their **sexual orientation** or **gender identities** are three times more likely to think about suicide than other teens. Adolescence is a time of experimentation and discovery. Teens who question their sexuality, or realize that they are gay, lesbian, or bisexual, have an even harder time in high school than straight students because they often feel like outcasts. This is also true for **transgender** teens who do not feel that they "fit" into the categories of male or female. Many have a hard time telling their parents about their sexuality. If they are rejected by their families, their suicide risk is even greater.

Control Over Something

When things feel overwhelming, it is easy to feel that you are not in control of what happens to you. This is especially true for traumatic experiences such as a death in the family, divorce, and abuse. Teens who think about suicide often express a need to be in control of something. They might not be able to prevent bad things from happening to them, but they can control whether they live or die. What suicidal teens might not realize is that while they cannot always control what happens in their lives, they can control how they respond to life events. Suicide prevents you from getting control of your life. It is a sign that a person is completely out of control.

"It's not like if you break your arm or get cancer. With that you get help. People care and they don't blame you for the broken arm. They can see that something is wrong and they understand. With mental illness, people think you can think yourself better and you are just not trying. They abandon you because of the things you do. But it's an illness in my head. Once I recognized that, once others recognized that, I could start to see straight, to get better."
Giselle, aged 16.

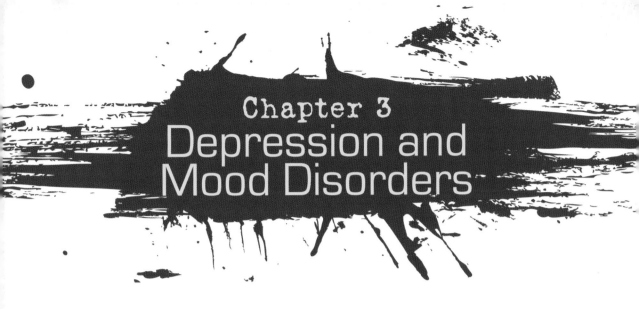

Chapter 3
Depression and Mood Disorders

There are some medical conditions that can make a person more likely to think about suicide. That does not mean that if you have one of these conditions, you will necessarily think about killing yourself. It also does not mean that thinking about suicide is a sign that you have a medical condition. It just means that some medical conditions can make people more likely to experience suicidal thoughts and behaviors.

What Is a Mood Disorder?

A mood disorder is a term that doctors and psychologists use to describe a pattern of thoughts and behaviors that is different from what we think of as "normal" thoughts and behaviors. It can be hard to tell when someone has a mood disorder, since mood disorders affect the brain, and we cannot see what goes on inside a person's brain. People are born with mood disorders. They can make life very challenging, but usually, they can be managed or treated so that a person can live a pretty normal life.

Sometimes I Feel "Moody"

Moodiness is a word that describes feeling cranky, grumpy, angry, or upset for no real reason. It is normal to feel this way from time to time. There are many things that affect our moods, including stress, how much sleep or exercise we get, or the foods we eat. A mood disorder, on the other hand, is a medical condition that makes people experience more negative feelings and thoughts than others, and these thoughts and feelings affect how well they function in life.

Depression

Depression is a mood disorder that makes a person feel so down, or depressed, that they have a hard time functioning. Depression is different from regular sadness, which is a healthy emotion that comes and goes as a result of things that happen in our lives. Depression makes you feel like you are moving through syrup. You want to sleep for weeks. You stop taking care of yourself. Signs of not taking care of yourself include not showering or brushing your teeth, leaving your hair a tangled mess, and eating a lot of unhealthy food. People who are depressed stop participating in their lives. They pull away from friends and family, preferring to lock themselves away in the dark. They spend a lot of time alone, feeling bad, thinking that their lives are going nowhere. Depression also makes you think that there is no hope in your life. It makes you feel helpless to do anything about your problems. Depression can make a person feel like there is no point in living.

"I Feel Depressed"

A lot of people say that they are "depressed" when something bad happens to them or when they feel sad for a few days. Depression is more than that. A person has to feel really down most of the time and unable to bounce back, in order to be diagnosed as truly depressed. But feeling down from time to time is a normal, healthy, human experience.

At least one in eight people suffer from depression at some point during their teen years.

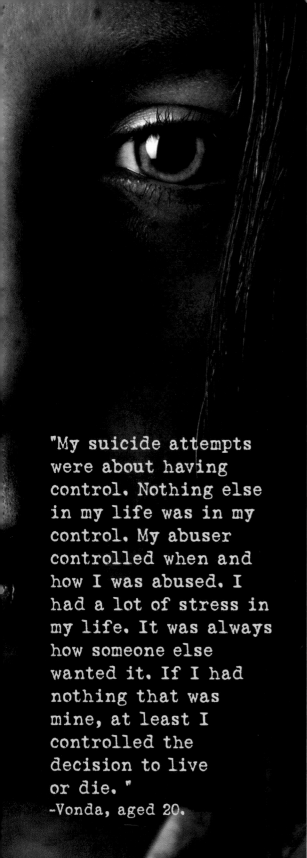

"My suicide attempts were about having control. Nothing else in my life was in my control. My abuser controlled when and how I was abused. I had a lot of stress in my life. It was always how someone else wanted it. If I had nothing that was mine, at least I controlled the decision to live or die. "
-Vonda, aged 20.

Bipolar Disorder

Bipolar disorder is a mood disorder that makes people experience emotional extremes, which affect their behavior. People who have bipolar disorder experience periods of intense happiness and unusual behavior, which is described as "mania." During a manic period, a person may seem elated, hyper, and unstoppable. Bipolar disorder also makes people experience emotional lows, which are short-term depressions. During a depressive episode, people with bipolar disorder show the usual signs of depression. They can become hard to talk to, or might seem like they do not care if they live or die.

Post-traumatic Stress Disorder

Post-traumatic stress disorder (PTSD) is a normal response to extremely stressful life events. PTSD can prevent people from living their lives, which is why it is classified as a mood disorder. Some examples of stressful events that might cause a person to suffer from PTSD are car accidents, abuse, war, and natural disasters. People with PTSD have trouble concentrating, sleeping, and sometimes controlling anger.

Mood Disorders and Suicide

So what does all of this have to do with suicide? All of these mood disorders can make people more vulnerable to suicidal thoughts. Depression is an illness that clouds the way people think. It makes people feel so bad for so long that they might start to look for a way to end their suffering. PTSD is linked to suicide for the same reason. Bipolar disorder is linked to suicide because of the depressive episodes that are common with this disorder, but also because it makes people behave rashly. For people who are suffering, suicide may seem like a way out. Teens are more vulnerable to mood disorders because the teenage years are a time of intense change. Teenagers do not have the life experience to cope with feelings in the way that adults do.

Mood disorders make it hard to build solid emotional foundations.

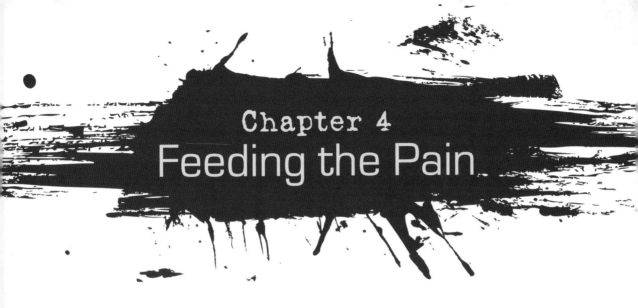

Chapter 4
Feeding the Pain

You do not have to have a mood disorder to be vulnerable to suicide ideation. Anyone can have suicidal thoughts, feelings, and behaviors. Many times, wanting to end your life comes from feeling overwhelmed by a situation or event, or many events. There are several other factors that can contribute to feeling unable to deal with life.

Substance Abuse

Substance abuse is the heavy use of drugs and/or alcohol to deal with difficult feelings or experiences. Having one or two drinks, when you are of legal age, is not substance abuse. Substance abuse means excessive use of drugs or alcohol as a way of coping with bad feelings. Substance abuse is not a healthy coping mechanism. It may temporarily numb pain or dull memories, but it does not make anything go away. People who abuse drugs or alcohol often feel even worse about their problems when they return to a **sober** state.

Experimentation

Adolescence is a time when many people experiment with alcohol. Many adolescents and teens experience drunkenness long before they are of legal drinking age. Since it is against the law to drink before the legal drinking age, many teens experiment with alcohol in unsafe, unsupervised conditions. This can be dangerous, especially in the case of overdose. Being drunk or high can also put you at risk for other dangers, such as assault, date rape, and other forms of violence. In other words, experimenting can open you up to problems that you are not prepared to deal with, which can make you turn to drugs and alcohol in an effort to escape.

A Vicious Cycle

One of the problems with drugs and alcohol is that they can become very **addictive**. It becomes increasingly difficult to stop using them. People who are addicted to drugs or alcohol experience feelings of helplessness. They become less and less able to "get through" a single day without being drunk or high. It is very hard to function with regular life this way. Going to school or work and doing homework become overwhelming tasks when you are drunk or high. Feeling overwhelmed is usually why people with drug or alcohol problems continue to abuse.

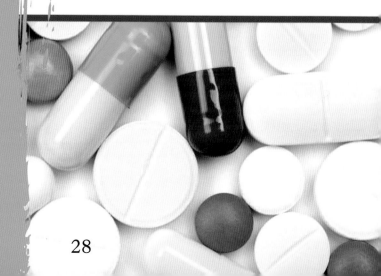

Downward Spiral

While some people may turn to drugs and alcohol to deal with larger problems, over time these addictions make them less able to cope with normal life. The original problems that the person was trying to escape from are still there, and the person still has to find a way to face them; but that is harder to do when dealing with an addiction on top of everything else. Eventually, they will need to seek treatment for addiction through a **rehabilitation** program, counseling, and group support such as Alcoholics or **Narcotics Anonymous**.

Risky Behavior

Addiction is an extreme example of what can happen with drugs or alcohol. Obviously, not everyone who tries drugs or alcohol becomes addicted. However, by lowering **inhibitions**, drinking and drug use can make you take risks that you would not normally take when sober. This can be dangerous because these substances can lead to poor judgment calls. People often make bad decisions when they are high or drunk, decisions that they later regret. Some examples of risky behavior include physical stunts, having unsafe, unprotected sex, and impaired driving.

Substance Abuse and Suicide

When you are under the influence of drugs or alcohol, you care less about what happens to you. This is true any time you are drunk or high, but it is especially true of prolonged substance abuse. Alcohol is a depressant, which means that it makes you feel down and lowers your energy. It clouds your thoughts, making it harder to think clearly and make wise decisions.

Over a period of time, using drugs or alcohol can put you at risk for serious depression. A person who is depressed may try to deal with their feelings by using more drugs and alcohol, which makes the depression more intense. They may also feel that they are powerless to fight their addiction, particularly if they have tried to quit and failed. Most suicide attempts are made under the influence of drugs or alcohol.

Being Bullied

Substance abuse is not the only problem that can feed into suicide ideation. Being bullied contributes to feelings of worthlessness and helplessness, and can lead to depression. Victims can feel so intimidated by the bullying that they are afraid to go to school. They may also feel isolated, or like no one can help them. Over time, victims of bullying may start to think about suicide as a way to escape their **tormenters**.

Family Relationships

Some teens who suffer from suicidal thoughts and feelings have problems in their families. Teens who are physically, emotionally, or sexually abused by family members feel very frightened and alone. They might not know who to turn to or how to make the abuse stop. This can lead to depression and unhealthy coping mechanisms, such as self-injury and drug or alcohol abuse. It can also lead to suicide ideation.

Constant fighting, tension, or abuse can make some teens think about suicide as a way to end strife.

"Everybody asks 'why did you do it' and I don't know.
It sounds stupid. Does there always have to be a
reason why?"
Courtney, aged 16.

Chapter 5
Warning Signs

People who are thinking about committing suicide usually send out warning signs before they make an attempt to end their lives. Unfortunately, these signs can be difficult to read, especially if someone is hiding away and refusing to talk. It is very important to pay attention if someone you know is showing any suicidal warning signs.

Early Signs

Most people experience a period of depression before they look to suicide as a solution. They may sleep a lot or not sleep at all. Often, they cut themselves off from friends and family by staying in their rooms and quitting sports teams or clubs that once gave them pleasure. Talking about suicide is another sign that someone might be thinking about ending his or her life. It might not be an obvious statement, such as "I want to die." If a friend says this, do not brush it off as a joke or an effort to get attention. Always take it seriously when someone talks about committing suicide.

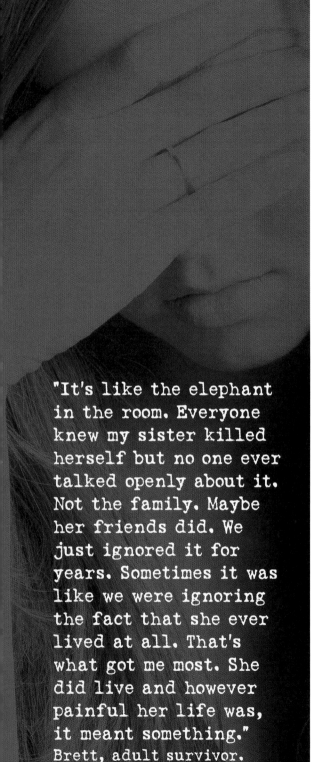

"It's like the elephant in the room. Everyone knew my sister killed herself but no one ever talked openly about it. Not the family. Maybe her friends did. We just ignored it for years. Sometimes it was like we were ignoring the fact that she ever lived at all. That's what got me most. She did live and however painful her life was, it meant something."
Brett, adult survivor.

Making a Plan

When someone makes a plan to die, they are in serious trouble and need help right away. Here are some signs that someone might be making a plan to die:

- dropping out of school

- buying a weapon, such as a gun

- putting things in order, such as making an informal will, writing letters to the people they care about, making sure that any responsibilities are tied up

- hoarding, or collecting, medications, such as painkillers or sleeping pills

- showing a sudden improvement in mood or cheering up out of the blue

- making direct statements such as "I'm going to kill myself" or "I want to die"

Reaching Out

It is common for people who are suicidal to let their plans "slip" to a friend. This might be one last desperate cry for help. Friends are often sworn to secrecy, but suicide is not a secret you should keep. It is very important that you get an adult involved. You cannot prevent your friend from being mad at you for sharing their secret, but even if your friend is mad, at least they will be alive.

"Why Me?"

After a suicide, it is common for friends and family to experience intense guilt. They blame themselves for not stepping in sooner or for not reading the warning signs. Sometimes, it is impossible to stop someone who has decided to end their life, especially if the warning signs are not obvious. Some suicides happen very suddenly, so there are no warning signs to read or interpret. Just making the effort to show someone that you care can make a huge difference to someone who has lost hope. You are not responsible for saving anyone's life, but you are responsible for reaching out to someone who is in trouble.

"It's very frustrating when I kept asking all these people to help me and I felt like I was being ignored...I hated being so depressed. I would do anything to feel better. After going through a series of crises, suicide felt like my only way out of this constant darkness. Thanks to my family, I'm in a much better place today, however, the work is ongoing to avoid going back to the bottom."
Lisa, formerly suicidal adult

Chapter 6
Seeking Help

Suicidal thoughts and feelings are not things that you should try to handle on your own. If you feel suicidal or if you are worried about a friend, you need to get help right away. Suicide is an emergency situation, and it is better to act before it is too late.

Asking for Help

When you are suicidal, it can be very hard to think straight. You may think that killing yourself makes perfect sense. It is very important that you reach out for help. You might think that no one would notice if you died and that the world would go on just fine without you. You are wrong. It might be hard for you to see now. Think of some people that you might be able to count on right now such as a parent, a friend's parent, a teacher, a counselor, a doctor, or a neighbor. If you feel like you might take action to end your life right now, you need help immediately. Call 9-1-1 or call a crisis line. Do not wait for these feelings to pass.

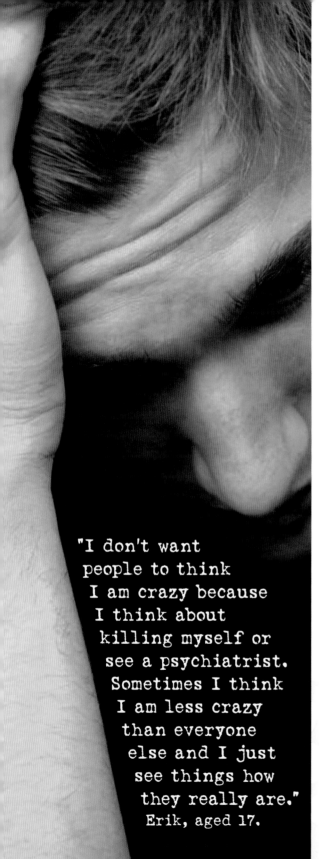

"I don't want
people to think
I am crazy because
I think about
killing myself or
see a psychiatrist.
Sometimes I think
I am less crazy
than everyone
else and I just
see things how
they really are."
Erik, aged 17.

What Comes Next?

The person you talk to might be shocked or surprised to hear what you have to say. Try not to worry about that. The important thing is taking care of yourself. The person you tell might need a bit of time to take in your news. No matter what happens, you need to focus on getting the support you need right now. If the person you tell does not come through for you, talk to someone else. Do not give up. After your conversation, you might be encouraged to visit a doctor or counselor. That is a really good idea. A doctor or counselor will ask you questions about your feelings that might be hard to answer. Take your time. Talking about your feelings is a sign that you want to feel better. Talking means that you are coping with your feelings.

Recovery Time

Recovering from suicidal thoughts and feelings can take some time, so be patient. Everyone is different, and there is no right way to heal. Over time, with the help of a doctor or counselor, and the support of friends and family, you will start to see that there is a lot of value in your life. You might need to make some changes to the way you deal with difficult emotions. This can involve working with a counselor, taking medication, and learning coping tools that work for you. You might also try group therapy, since it can be good to spend some time with others who have "been there."

Healing with Time

Healing does not happen overnight. It might take a while for you to start feeling better, but things will get easier eventually. You might still have suicidal thoughts once in a while. Try not to panic, but always get help when you feel like ending your life. It might be a good idea to make a list of names and numbers that you can call when you feel really upset. As you learn how to cope with difficult feelings, you will learn to express your pain in healthy ways. One of these ways might be taking up a form of art, such as painting, drawing, or photography. You might also find that yelling into a pillow when you feel upset is really helpful to you. Remember, this is your recovery so you need to learn what works best for you and stick with it.

Helping a Friend

Remember, it is always an emergency when someone wants to die. Pay attention. Try not to upset your friend by asking them a lot of questions. Approach the topic gently and in private. Use a quiet voice. Do not give your friend **ultimatums**, such as: "I won't be your friend if you don't get help." It is also important that you do not tell your friend to cheer up or that they have a lot to be thankful for. Lecturing will not help your friend right now. What will help is showing that you care, so reach out, listen, and try to be patient.

Another important thing to remember is that some people make a second attempt to commit suicide a few months after their first attempt. They might have received a lot of help right after their first attempt, but as they showed signs of improvement, the support might have gone away. That is why it is so important for friends and family to keep checking in on the person who attempted suicide.

People who have tried to commit suicide need friends who won't shy away when things get tough.

What Else Should I Know?

It is really challenging to know that a friend has tried to take his or her own life. You probably have a lot of questions. Good for you for being such a caring friend that you want to learn more. It is a good idea to talk to a professional counselor, a minister, or a teacher if you are feeling upset or confused. Whatever you do, do not try to hold it inside.

I Lost Someone

Losing someone to suicide is one of the hardest things you can experience. You probably feel lost, scared, and confused. You might also feel angry, guilty, and shocked. It is always hard when a friend or family member dies, but it is even harder when the death is a result of suicide. That is because many people do not talk openly about suicide. In some cultures, suicide is a **taboo** topic, so it can be really hard to get the help you need if no one will talk to you about it.

You should not feel ashamed about needing help after losing someone. It is common for survivors to have nightmares and anxiety.

41

Chapter 7
Coping Toolbox

If you are struggling with suicidal thoughts and feelings, it is a really good sign that you are reading this book. You are brave for realizing that you need help. A lot of people feel afraid or worried when they hear the word "counseling." That is totally normal. You probably feel anxious because you do not know what counseling really involves. You might also feel **skeptical** about a stranger being able to help you. Counseling is more or less a conversation between you and someone who is trained to talk to people about their problems. Counselors work with people to determine the main reasons for their unhappiness, and offer ways of dealing with life in healthy, positive ways.

Eating healthy foods can make you feel healthier. This makes it easier to cope.

Then What?

If you have been feeling depressed and suicidal for a long time, or if you have tried to kill yourself, your doctor might want you to take medication. This might be a short-term treatment, or you might need medication for the long term. These medications may have some side effects, which are ways that your body responds to new substances. Your doctor will go over the side effects with you, but a few that you might want to look out for are headaches, nausea, sleepiness, dizziness, and increased suicidal feelings.

Staying Safe

You might continue to have suicidal thoughts once in a while. It is a good idea to have a plan for what to do when that happens. Try making a safety plan that will work for you. You might want to break it down into steps. For example:

1) Ask yourself: "Am I in danger right now? Do I need to call for help?" Call emergency services or a crisis line if you feel like you might hurt yourself.

2) Take deep breaths and count to ten.

3) Call a friend. Have the number ready so you do not have to look for it.

Those are just a few steps that might help you, but you might think of other things you can do when you feel suicidal. Whatever you do, do not wait for the feeling to pass. Reach out for help.

Hot Topics Q&A

Q: What do I do about a friend who constantly threatens suicide? Do I take her seriously?

A: Yes, you should always take it seriously when someone talks about suicide. Even if your friend isn't moments away from trying to kill herself, talking about suicide is a sign that she needs help. Ask her what's going on and tell her that you're there for her. Offer to go speak to a parent or guidance counselor at school. You might also try giving her the number to a crisis line.

Q: I don't think anyone will care if I live or die. Why should I care about them?

A: It's hard to see clearly when you're depressed. You might not believe it, but there are a lot of people in your life who love you and want you to be safe. You might see ending your life as a solution to your problems, but just think of the pain you will inflict on the people who care. You will leave them with a lifetime of grief and sadness. You might not think that they can help you, but if you open up to them about the way you feel, you might be surprised by what they have to say.

Q: My grandma says suicide is a sin. But my friend says it is noble. Why does he think this?

A: There is no real right answer to this question. People have very strong beliefs when it comes to suicide, and everyone is entitled to their beliefs—including you. Many religions frame suicide as a sin, but many people believe the opposite. Psychologists would tell you that suicide is wrong because it prevents people from finding help for their problems, and that no problem is worth killing yourself over.

Q: I lost my dad to suicide. He died last year, but I just can't get over it. What should I do?

A: Losing someone to suicide is one of the most upsetting things that can happen to you. It's a really good idea to speak to somebody about your grief, such as a counselor or other trusted adult. It will hurt for a long time, but with the right support, your pain will give way to happy memories. Try to keep track of how you feel each day. You might want to explore your feelings in a journal to help you remember. If you think you are slipping into a depression, or if you feel really "stuck" in your grief, or if you start thinking about ending your own life, it's definitely time to speak to a counselor.

Q: My friend cries a lot, sometimes over silly things like sad songs. Is that normal? Is she depressed?

A: There is a difference between sensitivity and depression. If your friend has always cried a lot, then you probably shouldn't worry—but you can always ask her if she's okay if you're concerned. The thing to watch out for is a major change in behavior. Did something upsetting recently happen in her life? If you're not sure, you might want to ask.

Other Resources

Suicide is a complicated topic. It is always a good idea to talk to an adult if suicide has touched your life in some way. Here are other resources that might help answer some of the questions you might have right now. The Web sites will contain useful information no matter which country you live in, but telephone numbers and referral services will be country-specific.

In the United States

American Foundation for Suicide Prevention

www.afsp.org

This site comes from a foundation that works to spread awareness about suicide. Get tips on how to help yourself or a friend. Information on recovery after someone close to you takes their life is also useful.

TeensHealth: Suicide

http://kidshealth.org/teen/your_mind/mental_health/suicide.html#

This page explains what depression feels like, why it is important to reach out for help, and how to tell if a friend might be suicidal.

Suicide Awareness Voices of Education (SAVE)

www.save.org

SAVE provides information on suicide, with a focus on prevention. For help in an emergency, call the National Suicide Prevention Lifeline at this toll-free phone number 1-800-273-8255.

Boys Town National Hotline
1-800-448-3000

This crisis line is for teens and parents who need help with any problem. The counseling service is free of charge, and available 24-hours-a-day, seven-days-a-week.

GLBT National Youth Talkline
1-800-246-PRIDE (1-800-246-7743)

This hotline offers telephone peer counseling to gay, lesbian, bisexual, transgendered, and questioning youth, Monday to Friday from 5-9 pm (Pacific Time).

In Canada
Centre for Suicide Prevention
www.suicideinfo.ca/

This site offers help for people in crisis, as well as people who want to learn more. Note that this is a Canadian site, so not all of the information will apply to people living in the United States.

Kids Help Phone
1-800-668-6868

www.kidshelpphone.ca

A Canadian crisis line. Professional counselors can answer any questions and give you referrals to services in your area.

Other Resources
ReachOut: Suicide
http://au.reachout.com/find/issues/mental-health-difficulties/suicide

ReachOut is an organization that helps youth deal with many difficult issues, including abuse, self-injury, mental health problems, and suicide. ReachOut is an Australian organization, so not all of the information will apply to people living in the United States, Canada, and other parts of the world.

Glossary

acknowledge To accept or admit

addictive Something that is habit forming and very hard to quit

Aspergers syndrome A disorder where people have difficulties interacting

coping mechanism Behavioral tools that people use to relieve stress or pain

gender identities The genders people identify with including male, female, both, or in-between

hormones Substances produced by your body that influence behavior and mood

inhibitions The feelings that make someone self-conscious

insecure Not confident or assured

intense Strong or extreme

isolation Keeping separate or apart

mood disorders Medical conditions that affect moods and the way people think and act

morally In keeping with ideas of what is right and wrong

Narcotics Anonymous An organization that helps recovering drug addicts

phenomenon A fact that exists but for which there is no explanation

predictable Something that occurs the way it is expected

psychologists People who study the human mind, emotions, and behavior

rehabilitation To restore to a normal, healthy state through therapy

sexual orientation The sex a person is attracted to

skeptical Not easily convinced

sober Not influenced by drugs or alcohol

stereotype A widely held but oversimplified view or image or someone or something

taboo A social or religious custom prohibiting something

therapy Treatment designed to heal or relieve a disorder

tormentors Those who cause suffering

transgender Someone who identifies with a gender different from their biological sex

traumatic Something that is emotionally disturbing or distressing

ultimatums Strong demands

vulnerable Susceptible or easy to harm

Index